TRIUMPH
over
GRIEF

TurnKey
press

by

Joyce Smith Williams

Triumph Over Grief

ISBN 0-9740030-8-5

Published in the United States by

TurnKey Press
2525 W. Anderson Lane, Suite 540
Austin, Texas 78757
Tel: 512.407.8876
Fax: 512.478.2117
E-mail: info@turnkeypress.com
Web: www.turnkeypress.com

Cover design and layout by Gestalt Design Studio

First Edition: May 2003

10 9 8 7 6 5 4 3 2 1

TRIUMPH OVER GRIEF

by
Joyce Smith Williams

may you always triumph!

Joyce Williams

Table of Contents

PART III:
Moving to the Light

PROLOGUE

August 2002

On Tuesday, I wake, slide from the warm covers and thread my way from bedroom to bath. Minutes later, more comfortable, I return to my bed to relapse into sleep. But I twist and turn, can't get comfortable. What am I going to do with this story that demands to be told? Sleep is impossible – or so my experience informs me. I sneak a look at my bedside clock – 3:25 A.M. My internal voice says you might as well get up and free the monster.

Refusing to turn on the light, I reluctantly make my way in the darkness through the kitchen, through the dining room, through the living room, into my office. My eyes, so recently freed from cataracts, blink as I switch on the desk lamp. Perhaps when I've let the story out I can snuggle back under the covers for some restful sleep. In the darkness of the predawn, I begin the story of a life-shattering phone call.

Reluctantly, I allow my mind to regress to September 17, 1985 – a date indelibly printed on my mind. The call changed the course of my life and my family's life. Am I willing to reveal what transpired that September evening? At least reveal it as I remember it? Will I be able to make my family and friends understand the terror, the pain, and the isolation we felt? Will they consciously or unconsciously assume I wish to be seen as a victim? Why does the evaluation of a counselor-seven years ago-still infuriate me? The statement he wrote: "Joyce has used grief as a trump card."

1

I rehearse the victim question, and others pelt my like a prickly rain. Questions, always questions-they come easy. Answers are elusive. Will my senior-citizen status be a barrier to communication as I tell this story? Can individuals, some of them decades younger than I am, understand the hysteria of AIDS in 1985? Hysteria that threatened my job, doomed me to the burden of a secret, and snatched my best friend, my lover, and my confidant from me? Will they believe the death certificate, which read "heart attack," could have read "died of a broken heart?"

Seventeen years later, I continue to ponder questions that have dominated my thinking, disturbed my sleep, and screamed to be answered. Why do the memories of that call not fade? Why do I continue to hear that anguished voice in my waking hours and in my sleep? Why do I recall the smell of her perfume and visualize features of her pale face, distorted by pain, yet serene? One question dominates. What empowered my daughter to survive, knowing that her illness was responsible for the death of one child and would soon snuff out her own life, then the life of her firstborn?

In December of 1987, Luke and Joyce make a trip to their
Georgia property to select a site on the Chickamauga Creek for
their retirement home. This land, still undeveloped, has been
in the Williams family for almost two hundred years.

Matt, at about age three, loves to
be Superman.

Lydia – about age three.

Lydia holds Bryan, a frail infant who lived with constant pain; the first child in Dallas County to die of AIDS.

Lydia's new look - after her braids were snipped.

On a visit to Dallas, Joyce and Lydia share a cup of tea.

PART I:
Raging Waters

*Tho' the angry surges roll
on my tempest driven soul,
I am peaceful for I know
Wildly tho' the winds may blow,
I've an anchor safe and sure
And in Christ I shall endure.*

"MY ANCHOR HOLDS"
by W. C. Martin and D.B. Towner

CHAPTER ONE
Exposed

My private sorrow appears on the front page of The New York Times
and The Dallas Morning News

* * *

Fall 1992

The phone rang in my office about 9 A.M.

"Joyce, are you aware that your family's story is on the front page
of The New York Times and The Dallas Morning News?" a familiar
voice asked. I felt faint.

"No," I hesitated. " But I knew this time would come. Thanks for
calling. I'll drive to the post office and get the paper."

I grabbed my purse and dashed out the door. My secretary looked
up in surprise. "I'll be back soon." The post office was only two miles
away, but the drive seemed to take hours. On arrival, I pulled into a
parking slot, left the motor running, and put money in the newspaper
stand. I pulled the door down and took out the paper.

In the upper left hand corner of The Dallas Morning News was the
headline. Somehow I made it back to the car. My body was not coop-
erating. Inside, I remembered a recent phone call. My son-in-law had
called to say he planned "to go public" and that he "was tired of living
in secret." I did not understand the intensity of his feelings nor his need

to tell his story. For me, a very private person, I felt my innermost pain was being exposed to the world. Why had I not protested during the discussion about "going public?" I took a deep breath, looked around to see who might be watching, and read the entire article. Tears streamed down my face.

Now I had no choice. I was an administrator in a one hundred thirteen-year-old private school in San Antonio. Now I must tell my staff. At this point only my secretary knew the AIDS story. I walked back into the office and put the newspaper on her desk.

"Sue," I said, as I pointed to the left hand corner, "please don't talk about the news story."

With trembling hands and a heavy heart, I walked into my office, closed the door, and began to write.

TO THE MONTESSORI STAFF:

I wish I could talk with each of you personally. But time does not permit. So my hope is that in some small way this letter will answer some questions for you. I am aware that many of you know of the recent publicity with regard to my daughter Lydia's illness and death.

The two of us-Lydia and I-had discussed the possibility that the news of her infection would someday be made public. If I understood her correctly, it was her wish that her story not be made public as long as her son Matt lived. Understanding her desire for privacy, I respected that wish. As mothers and teachers who know children, I'm sure you will understand.

Today the story is on the front page of The New York Times and The Dallas Morning News; last night it was on the NBC evening news and this morning on the "Today" show.

So, because you have been my family for almost twenty years, I'd like to give you some information that you may never read or hear on the news.

Many of you remember October 1982, when Lydia was pregnant and hospitalized in San Francisco. As soon as I knew Lydia was in trouble, I left school, flew to Dallas, and met Luke. We flew to San Francisco, rented a car, and hastily made our way through traffic to Mount Zion Hospital.

Lydia was swollen almost beyond recognition. Death appeared to be imminent.

In a heroic effort to save Lydia's life, and the life of her unborn child, doctors ordered many pints of blood and various blood products. Hours later, Matt, a small, grey infant who registered a six on the APGAR scale, was born. Luke and I had a second grandson. Would we be able to keep him?

When Matt was three, Lydia had a second son, Bryan. Born prematurely, he weighed only three pounds. One evening, when Bryan was five months old, Lydia got a call from the blood bank in San Francisco.

"Mrs. Allen, one of the blood transfusions you received three years ago contained the HIV virus."

For the next five months, my husband Luke and I watched Bryan die slowly of AIDS, a disease that causes excruciating pain-physical, mental, and emotional.

Bryan's death certificate read "Leukemia"; true, but it was secondary to the HIV infection. We buried Bryan knowing two other family members would follow-Lydia and Matt.

The timeframe was uncertain. Lydia lived much longer than we dared to hope. She was on two experimental drugs, AZT and DDI, and a host of other medications-many involving severe side effects. She had shingles some twelve to fourteen times.

For months Lydia's health steadily declined. She was in bed most of the time in much pain, yet she made the final weeks of her life count. As you know, I took a leave of absence and felt privileged to be with her that last month. There were several things she requested I do for her. Most were accomplished.

Soon after Christmas of 1992, Matt was told that his mom was dying. Aware of his own condition, he found the news extremely disturbing. Facing Bryan's death, for him, had been agonizing. Thankfully, with the help of a wonderful therapist, he understood as best a nine-year-old is able.

I regret I could not be more open with you. I hedged on questions and sobbed in secret. I know that with the disease of AIDS there is still a lot of misunderstanding. In order to protect Lydia and Matt from further discrimination, Luke and I shared our family problem with very few people. With Scott's decision to go public, there is no longer any need for silence.

*   *   *

I regret that the timing of this announcement has come almost simultaneously with the announcement of my retirement. To be able to lose myself in my work here has probably helped me maintain my sanity. I know there have been days when I have not functioned well. Again, you stood in the gap; you gave much more than your job description required. Thanks!

I have great faith in each of you and know that as you always do, you will go the extra mile. I appreciate it.

At this moment I have no idea what tomorrow holds, nor the months ahead. Please bear with me as I continue to "walk through the valley of the shadows."

I love and respect you as friends, teachers, and professionals. May God bless and guide each of you.

Much love,

Joyce

*   *   *

My words to my staff were on paper. How would they be received?

11

CHAPTER TWO

Wearing the Scarlet Letter

In the height of the AIDS terror of the 1980's, how does a young mother cope with the fact that she is HIV-positive and has infected her two young sons?

* * *

Lydia shared her pain in an anonymous letter to the Baptist Standard.

When teaching phonics to my preschooler, we started at the beginning of the alphabet. "This is the letter A," I said. "Do you know a word that begins with A?" The poignant reply came, "A is for AIDS."

So it is in our lives: A is for AIDS. It is the beginning and ending of every facet of our existence. We are the new untouchables.

I had become infected with the AIDS virus by a blood transfusion while still pregnant with my first child. As a result, our baby also contracted the virus. Although I was frequently ill and fatigued, I passed it off as being "the new-mother syndrome."

Our baby was quite ill, requiring weekly trips to the doctor, and I blamed much of my exhaustion on stress. Having no idea that I was carrying the AIDS virus, two years after the birth of my first child, I became pregnant again.

Our second child was premature and also had multiple medical problems. When the new baby was five months old, I received a call from the blood bank that had supplied the blood for my transfusions. They said the donor who had given the blood for my transfusions had AIDS.

My world started reeling. As soon as I heard the words, all the events of the past three years came into focus with a searing clarity-the children's inability to stay well, the doctor's frequent head-shaking and statements: "This is rare. The medicine should have worked."

Within two months, I had lost most of what constituted my world. Our baby was in critical condition with days to weeks to live. My husband had lost his job and career when his employer found out that his family had been touched by AIDS. Our older child had to be removed from day-care. We were asked not to return to our church. Our confidentiality had been breached, and as word spread throughout our community, we quickly fled and relocated in another town. We were too terrified to risk harassment and persecution.

Several months after our move, our baby died, and the second phase of my isolation began. This isolation was self-imposed, by fear. The few relationships I have had are superficial and almost totally based on fabrication. How could I truthfully answer simple questions: "Why did you move here?" "What was wrong with your baby?" I couldn't talk about the fact my heart was breaking every time I looked at my little son. I couldn't share that my marriage was fragmenting from the incredible stress in our lives. I couldn't "act sick" lest someone get suspicious, so I hid my symptoms and pain.

I didn't dare reveal anything about the severity of our son's illness lest my child be totally ostracized from all socialization. I couldn't even contact former co-workers to explain why I had suddenly disappeared. I was in a new city with no friends, no church, no "home" (we had left "home"), no job, a struggling marriage, a very sick child, and the grief over the loss of our baby. I had never been so alone in my life.

We reached out to a local church. The pastor was supportive, but when he asked parents about the possibility of our child attending Sunday school, the parents said no. We do not attend church now. The rejection runs too deep.

To Christians I would say that AIDS cripples not only the body, but the heart. At a time when the AIDS victim is dealing with death and dying, heavy financial burdens, and physical debilitation, they need support, care, and concern-not rejection! If there was ever a time to reach out and touch the "lepers" of our day, it is now.

I wear the Scarlet A. I keep it well-hidden. You may never see me cry or realize from my appearance that I have been infected by the virus. Nevertheless, I have been shattered. I need love, compassion, and community to help me make it from day to day. I have done nothing immoral or illegal to contract this disease, but those who have hurt just as deeply as I. Their needs are great or greater than mine for a compassionate and loving response to people with AIDS."

CHAPTER THREE
Bryan

What DOES tomorrow hold? Or the months ahead? Are my days to be consumed only with memories? Such as the ones of my infant grandson, Bryan, the first to die of AIDS? In spite of time, some memories do not fade.

* * *

The first anniversary of Bryan's death

The sun shone brightly as the car moved through the quiet streets of Brownwood, Texas and came to a stop in front of the florist shop. Lydia, her dad, and I waited as Scott, our son-in-law, climbed from the car and strode toward the door.

"I'll only be a minute."

I sneaked a quick look at Luke sitting behind the wheel and realized my tears were about to spill over. Every day since the phone call had seemed like a year. Had it only been five months? My grandmother pain, my worry, and my grief bubbled under the surface of my consciousness like a volcano.

Soon, the door of the florist shop flung open and Scott emerged. He carried a bouquet of balloons tied with brightly-colored ribbons bobbing in the breeze.

My heart pounded and seemed too big for my body. Did we have to participate in this ritual? Was it really time to make our way to the cemetery?

Luke, my husband of forty years, now a greying grandfather, started the car and headed for the highway. We drove in silence, each of us immersed in private thoughts.

...Only ten months old. Such a short life. What a struggle from the beginning.

One year ago we had placed Bryan's tiny casket in the grave. But I could still smell the medication, feel Bryan's tiny body snuggle into my neck, and hear him cry out in pain as we rocked in the midnight darkness.

...Had my intuition been right? Would the gift – the one I had packed into the trunk of the car – be meaningful to Lydia and Scott on this anniversary? Would it convey how much Luke and I shared their grief?

The car slowed as we drove through this small West Texas town. I spotted the sign: Evergreen Gardens.

With his perfect sense of direction, Luke made a couple of turns and pulled to a stop beside a large headstone with the name MASSEY carved into the marble.

"Bryan's marker isn't ready yet," said Scott, as he broke the silence. "But it will go right there next to his granddad Massey's."

We nodded and climbed out of the car. Lydia stood silently, then pulled a folded piece of paper from her pocket. In an emotion-filled voice, she read from a Dickens poem used in Bryan's service.

> *"Can it be in a world so full and busy,*
> *The loss of one creature makes a void*
> *in any heart so wide and deep that nothing*
> *But the width and depth of vast eternity can fill it up?"*

Then Lydia paused, turned her head to conceal her tears, and began to untie the balloons. With the sun to our backs, we watched as the wind caught each balloon and carried it heavenward.

A silver balloon turned, twisted, and reflected the rays of the sun, even after the others had disappeared.

"Good-bye, Bryan. We love you!"

From the tiny gravesite, Luke and I made out way to the car, took our gift from the trunk, and placed it on the backseat. Following Bryan's death I had grappled with an idea. *Was it possible to put the words to a hymn used in his service on fabric? Could it become a picture?* I discussed the idea with one of my teachers, an expert in counted cross-stitch. She assured me it could be done.

"By February? In time for the first anniversary of Bryan's death?"

One January morning, the expert in counted cross-stitch peeked around my office door.

"Want to see it?"

I jumped from my chair and rushed to the door. The neatly framed cream-colored mat with robin's-egg blue lettering was finished. We packed it carefully in the trunk of my car.

* * *

Lydia and Scott returned to the car moments later, opened the back door, and lifted out the framed hymn. With tears streaming down their faces, they read the words:

BRYAN CALEB ALLEN
May 12, 1985 - February 2, 1986

In the land of the walking wounded,
In this desert of countless sorrows,
I will cling to his hand today
And fear not for tomorrow.

In my heart I have made this promise
And with this song, I declare my choice
I will walk where the Shepherd leads me
And heed no other voice.

In the chill of my darkest hour
I am saved from my deep despair
For the Father who loves his children
Hears my trusting prayer.

In my soul there is one light shining
from the flame of my true belief
And its embers cannot be quenched
Or robbed by any thief.

In the end we are not forgotten
and our journey is not in vain
For the Master who brought us here
will lead us home again.

– RANDY STONEHILL

As we waited for the emotions to wane, I looked into the brilliant blue sky and paid silent tribute. *Bryan, you are not forgotten. There will ALWAYS be special memories of you. Yes, Mr. Dickens, the loss of one creature does make a void in my heart so wide and deep that nothing but the width and depth of vast eternity can fill it up.* Perhaps there are bigger questions, Mr. Dickens. Several plagued me. *Can the faith of my childhood endure amid mounting doubts? Will this kind of pain damage my spirit? Can I spare time to grieve the loss of a ten-month-old when the living need every ounce of strength I have?*

* * *

18

WHO COULD KNOW?

Who could know in those long, brooding hours

When I sat with only you

Clasped next to me

Longing for blissful respite

That night should become my enemy

With sleep as elusive as shadows at dawn.

Who could know

That I would some hour yearn

To once again be pressed to wakefulness

By one small cry instead of loneliness.

– BY LYDIA ALLEN

CHAPTER FOUR
With a Grateful Heart

A minister knows how to bring comfort to parents and grandparents

* * *

March 14, 1988

Dr. A. M. Pennybacker
University Christian Church
Ft. Worth, TX 76110

Dear Dr. Pennybacker:

Two years ago you conducted the funeral service for our grandson, Bryan Caleb Allen. You ministered to our family in a more significant way than you could possibly know.

My reason for writing you at this time is to tell you of a dream that has become a reality. At a time when Matthew was having so much trouble accepting Bryan's death, Lydia looked for books to comfort and give hope. Finding none, she wrote a story for him called "I Miss My Little Brother." I was touched by the story and decided to get it printed.

Over a year ago I began working with Jean Rosow, a professional artist who lived here in San Antonio, to get the story illustrated. I wanted the pictures to convey ideas that children need in dealing with death. The

book came from the printer last Wednesday. Luke and I would like you to have a personal copy.

It is my dream, and Lydia's, that "I Miss My Little Brother" will someday be published and that it will help fill the void in the lives of families who have had a young child die.[1] Luke joins me in wishing for you the very best in using your gifts in continued ministry.

Sincerely,

Joyce Williams

CHAPTER FIVE
Luke

Because of AIDS, Luke and I couldn't leave Texas and be 1,500 miles away from Lydia, Scott, and Matt. Luke accepted a position with the Baptist Memorial Hospital System in San Antonio as their director of development. One of his first tasks was to plan and set up a Hospital Foundation. He submerged his grief in long, exhausting work days.

* * *

Then...

"Honey," Luke said as he shook me. "Wake up! I need to go to the hospital." Emerging from a sound sleep, I tried to clear my brain. *What did he say?*

"Luke, what's the matter?"

In the dim light I could see Luke's ashen-grey face contorted with pain.

"Just get dressed quickly," he advised. "I've already taken two nitro-glycerin tablets but they haven't helped."

I drove downtown, disregarding the speed limit. When we came to a red light, my rules-oriented husband said, "Run it." The tone of his voice gave me further reason to panic. When we reached the emergency room door, the medical personnel recognized the gravity of the situation and began immediate action. An IV was started and injections were given, but Luke's pain did not subside and his blood pressure continued to drop. Nurses and doctors worked furiously. After a quick phone call, the emergency room doctor stepped into the room carrying a clipboard.

"Mr. Williams, this is a very serious heart attack. I've spoken with your doctor, and he is bringing a cardiologist. In the meantime, he wants us to start TPA, a drug that could dissolve the blood clot. The sooner the medication is started, the less likely there will be permanent damage to the heart muscle. But, I must warn you that there could be side effects. In rare cases, this drug, which is a blood thinner, will cause hemorrhages in the brain. Now, I will leave you two to make a decision. If you decide TPA is what you want, you will need to sign this release."

My mind was not functioning. This couldn't be happening. God had promised he wouldn't give me more than I could bear. *My God, my God, why have you forsaken me?*

Luke was the strong one. The one everyone counted on in a time of crisis. Lydia needed him. She was losing her nine-year battle with AIDS. Matt, also HIV-positive, needed his granddad. Luke had held the family together when ten-month-old Bryan lost his battle with AIDS. I could not lose this man of God, my husband of forty-four years. Not on his sixty-sixth birthday.

Pale and obviously in pain, Luke looked deep into my eyes for what seemed like an eternity.

"I guess we don't have much choice, do we?"

Too emotional to speak, I shook my head and signed the release.

The drug was administered. Within minutes the blood pressure began to stabilize, the pain subsided, and the ashen-grey color faded. Still worried, I stepped into the hall to question the doctors about the possible side effects of TPA.

"Mrs. Williams, " the cardiologist said, "I've been giving this drug for years and I've never had a patient react. Relax and don't worry."

By 8:30 A.M. our daughters, Virginia and Lydia, had arrived from Dallas. Their dad was propped up in bed, smiling and almost pain-free. Luke's internist and the cardiologist checked him again.

"Doesn't look like we are needed around here now, but we will check back in."

Joy filled my heart and I breathed a prayer of thanks.

News spread quickly through the medical center that the newly-elected president of the Hospital Foundation had suffered a serious heart attack. Friends gathered; chaplains offered support; hospital administrators came and left. A private room near the intensive care unit was provided for our family and friends who had gathered. All seemed to be going well.

Suddenly a nurse appeared in the doorway and motioned to me.

"Mrs. Williams, please come with me. Your husband has just lost his ability to speak."

I raced to the intensive care unit and looked into Luke's face. He smiled, raised an eyebrow, and sank back into his pillow. Blood began gushing from his mouth and he lost consciousness.

Somehow I found my way back to the waiting room, devastated. Crumpled in the corner of the room, I needed to cry, but no tears would come.

* * *

Arranging their films on the viewing screen, the cardiologist asked the team of neurosurgeons to explain what had happened.

"Mrs. Williams, the drug TPA has done its work in dissolving the blood clot that caused your husband's heart attack. But you see the large dark areas on the film? Those indicate bleeding in the brain – bleeding so severe we cannot recommend making any attempt to alleviate the pressure."

My beloved Luke was dying. *Where was the God in whom I had placed my trust?*

* * *

Our son, David, arrived from Phoenix about 4 P.M. He, Lydia, Virginia, and I stood beside Luke's bed watching in disbelief. Lydia, a nurse, spoke softly to her brother.

"Dave, he'll be going soon. He was waiting for you to get here."

Then turning to her dad she said, "Dad, we're all here. It's okay, you can let go now. We love you. We'll meet you on the other side."

The line on the monitor went flat.

* * *

Appreciation

Memorial services can bring comfort.

November 1991
Dr. Jimmy R. Allen
5008 Arborlawn
Ft. Worth, TX 76110

Dear Jimmy,

Since Luke's funeral, I have been writing this letter in my mind. No words can express my appreciation for the support you and Wanda gave during those dark, difficult days.

Finding the piece of paper where Luke and I, just three weeks earlier, had recorded the kind of service both of us wanted was a gift. I thank God for his grace in providing that time of discussion and the judgment to write it down. You took that rough outline and put together a perfect service.

Somehow, through Luke's service, I came to understand how a person can have joy even when their heart is breaking. Now, I know that joy is possible, even in grief.

I'm so grateful I had presence of mind to make the arrangement to have the service video taped. I sent a copy to my mom and her cousin, Mrs. T.B. Maston, who were unable to attend. I find comfort in viewing the tape.

During the months since his death, I have become aware of the countless lives Luke touched, some in unique ways. After 44 years, I guess I took his accomplishments for granted. I'm grateful for the years we had together and had counted on at least 20 more.

As you know, Luke loved the young congregation at Woodland Baptist. Surely there is a way I can use what I learned from watching Luke all those years to contribute to that work. I became a member last month. I do not always have the finesse and patience to work behind the scenes as Luke did, but I'll work at it.

Virginia, Lydia, and I enjoyed our trip to see the fall leaves but found my mother in very bad shape when we got to Chattanooga. I was in no way prepared for the emotional trauma of going back home without Luke. I had done it many times before, but his time was different! The "firsts" seem to hit the hardest.

I've been reading "Creative Suffering" by Paul Tournier. Some chapters I must re-read, but I am looking for reassurance any place I can find it. Again, words are so inadequate. But thanks for all you have done.

Joyce

* * *

Memories

Writing – putting my thoughts on paper – has always been therapeutic. I joined a critique group and began to write. My friend Carol and I went to a nature writing workshop at the Yellowstone Institute in Yellowstone National Park. One day our assignment involved studying designs of lichen on rocks beside a stream. We were to let our imagination run free and see what surfaced.

Lichen-speckled rock beside the bubbling stream in Yellowstone created images in my mind. I see blooming flowers, a mini-garden of pressed blossoms, and an ancient animal just emerging from its cracked shell.

Water cascades over one surface, under another, and through narrow crevices into larger pools creating a happy humming sound – one that penetrates my memory. What is it I so enjoy about the lively sight and sound of the flow of water descending the waterway?

Suddenly, I am transported – I see again a small log cabin in the Smoky Mountain National Park near Gatlinberg. Once again I am a bride on my honeymoon. I walk across the swinging bridge over the restless stream to my handsome young groom who waits expectantly.

Sights, sounds, and smells whittle away the years – but memories remain.

* * *

Observing the Gospel According to Luke

All who knew him loved and admired Luke. One of his associates, a fellow minister, spoke these words at his memorial service.

I had read a Gospel from Luke for years in Sunday School and church

And I'd heard its truths preached countless times

Yet I saw a Gospel in the life of a man named Luke,
a man who also walked with Christ.

From this gentle man, I saw the beauty of a life of service to family,
friends, hospitals, orphanages, churches and a denomination.

I observed the life of a person who saw his existence as one sent
to do good in the name of Christ.

What a message he was to those of us who knew him

What courage he gave through his friendship
What guidance he gave through his gift of time and concern

What wisdom he gave to fellow ministers

What cheer he gave to us through that marvelous gift of humor
  a gift which spoke of hope, of joy that understood
  that Christ had indeed overcome the world.

What strength he gave as he bore his own cross
  while easing the burden of others.

Yes, I've heard the Gospel of Luke before.

But I saw it in this one who showed me Christ,
  a person whose deeds cause me to give glory to God
  for sending this man named Luke.

— BY AL STAGGS IN MEMORY OF LUKE E. WILLIAMS, JR. 1925-1991

CHAPTER SIX
A Tribute to Lydia

A friend sums up a courageous life and concludes with "Simple Gifts."

* * *

After a slow, painful, nine-year struggle with AIDS, I knew Lydia's death was just hours away. I sat beside her bed. She had been in a coma for two days and nights. My walk through the dark valley of the shadow was dream-like. Seven months earlier I had watched Luke die suddenly, within a few hours of a heart attack. Now I watched Lydia's life ebb away slowly. Fast or slow, dream or nightmare, death was death. The pain seemed unbearable. *Would life ever again have meaning?*

Never did I dream I would face Lydia's death without Luke by my side. Lydia was "Daddy's girl." At the time of her dad's funeral she called a family conference.

"I think I have six months to live," she told us.

Now those six months were gone. As I watched Lydia's labored breathing, I recalled efforts to comfort her after her dad's death.

"Lydia, I'm sorry your dad is not here for you. I know how much you relied on him."

"But Mom, it will be easier this way. Dad could never have watched me die. It is a comfort to know he will be waiting for me – probably playing with Bryan when I get there."

At about four in the afternoon, Lydia came out of the coma, sat up in bed, and looked around. Then she quietly lay back on her pillow and her breathing ceased.

* * *

The memorial service Lydia had planned was held at the Shiloh Terrace Baptist Church in Dallas at seven in the evening, "a time that would accommodate her friends." Her beloved friend, Maria Bellatoni, gave the tribute:

> *For Lydia*
>
> *"'Lord, make me an instrument of thy peace.*
> *Where there's despair, let me bring hope.*
> *Where there is darkness, light.*
> *Where there is sadness joy.'*

These words, attributed to St. Francis of Assisi, are beautiful when spoken, more beautiful when sung, MOST beautiful when lived. And HOW Lydia lived them.

She sought not so much to be consoled, as to console. To be understood, as to understand. She brought hope to us in our despair, despite her own. She brought light to others, especially children, in their darkness, forgetting her own grief. She brought joy where sadness lingered, smiling despite her own pain, convincing us she was alright, driving us crazy sometimes with her calm demeanor, her measured approach.

I will always remember Lydia by my side as I labored during the birth of my son. As I carried on in agony befitting my Italian heritage, hysterical, she repeated over and over, helping me to breathe, 'Hee, hee, hoo.' I wanted to punch her out.

...Lydia and I did a lot of reminiscing these last few weeks. When she felt strong enough, I'd drive her around White Rock Lake. Sometimes we'd sit on the grass. While staring at the sunlight on the water, or watching the

ducks, we'd talk of life and death, God and the hereafter, and always her love and concern for Matthew.

Lydia told me before Christmas she felt she was dying. We had ridden around my neighborhood looking at Christmas lights, which she usually enjoyed. When we stopped and sat in the driveway, she was silent for a long time. Finally, she said she felt her time here was drawing to a close. It was a feeling hard to describe, she said, because, after all, this was her 'first time around at dying." She sensed, simply, a diminishing of the life force. And, as usual for Lydia, she was right.

...Each of us here has our own treasure of memories – of Lydia, the precocious child; Lydia the long-haired darling of the campus; Lydia, the young wife and mother; the gentle nurse; the granddaughter; loved one; roommate; and friend.

We talked about my doing the tribute for her service. I will never forget the look of horror which crossed her face when I told her I would begin the tribute by singing, in a shaky, breathy voice, 'Somewhere Over the Rainbow.' Lydia didn't want a tribute – saying it would embarrass her. Then, I assured her I would try to be understated in my remarks. I told her that her life spoke for itself, that nothing more needed to be said. She paused, grinned and said, 'I can live with that.'

When I asked Lydia if there was anything she'd like me to say to you, she replied, 'Tell them how much I love them. Tell them what means the most to me is that we have been connected by love, so many of us, in so many ways. That's what is important to me.'

Lydia, an extraordinary person, a brilliant woman, brought us closer to the valley of love and delight. And she did it with true humility, thankful for the gifts given to her, without need of recognition for the way she changed lives.

It was a profound honor to know and love my friend Lydia Ann Williams Allen. Free now, and at peace, I believe she dwells in another realm of love and delight. I believe that in some way she has taken the hand of her beloved father, Luke, and has cradled and rocked her baby boy, Bryan – that the three of them together are held in the loving and open arms of God. 'For God shall wipe away all tears from their eyes; and there shall be no more death, neither sorrow, nor crying, neither shall there be any more pain; for the former things are passed away.' (Revelations 21:4) And God shall be with them, and be their God. Amen."

The one request Lydia made for her service was for the singing of the Shaker tune: "Simply Gifts."

'Tis the gift to be simple,
'Tis the gift to be free,
'Tis the gift to come down where we ought to be,
And when we find ourselves in the place just right,
We'll be in the valley of love and delight.

Our family secret was still closely guarded. AIDS was not mentioned at Lydia's funeral, although by this time many people who attended the memorial service had been told privately of the problem.

I thought I was ready to deal with my grief. But as I looked into Matt's eyes – a little guy who had watched his mom die, who knew his own condition, who was only a third grader – I stuffed my grief down and dared the tears to form.

In a poem, Lydia asks a poignant question.

Who will sing my song tomorrow?
Or will it be sung?
Who will show the sorrow
by singing to the young?

Will my song be sung tomorrow?
How can one be sure?
For when can a vision be taught?
How is a dream secured?

It does not matter – now I know
Whether taught or learned the song
The melody resides within
the lyrics – each his own.

CHAPTER SEVEN
Lydia's Legacy

In her living and in her dying, Lydia pointed the way to transcend life's losses. Shortly before her death, on an audiotape she prepared for her mom, Virginia, and David, Lydia recalled childhood experiences.

* * *

These are just things I want to say that are not particularly personal, but in a way, are very personal.

In my life, I've had lots of people who loved me, and for that I'm very, very grateful. From the time I was a little bitty girl, I knew I was loved. I remember our family vacations at Indian Rocks Beach, Florida, walking along the shore finding shells. When I was about four or five, Mom and Dad were walking down the beach and had gotten pretty far ahead of me. I could see them as I checked for shells. Suddenly, up washed a big conch shell with the conch still in it. I was so proud of that conch shell. It was like it had been delivered especially to me. The shell hadn't been there when Mom and Dad walked by, but was when I walked by. That fact seemed to make it all the more special to me.

I remember riding in our new green station wagon from our house in Birmingham to Grandma's in Chattanooga for Christmas 1956. Lying in the back of the station wagon, we all sang Christmas carols. I remember how warm and comfortable I felt looking up at the stars as we drove down the highway headed for a visit with both our Grandmas and all the excitement that went with it.

I'm not sure, but I think that was the Christmas I found out who Santa Claus really was. I had been put to bed on the couch in the living room. The grown-ups had been waiting for me to go to sleep and I guess they thought I was asleep. Somehow or other, my suspicions had been raised, or maybe it was the anticipation of Christmas itself, but I was still awake and I remember seeing the grown-ups tiptoeing around and putting presents under the tree. Then I knew who Santa Clause really was. BUT, it never disturbed me or bothered me because I knew how much my parents and grandparents must have loved my sister, brother, and me to tiptoe around and play that charade.

Even as a very, very little girl I remember having faith – knowing that there was something larger than me. I was standing in the yard of our house on Indian Trail (in Chattanooga) looking up at the sky. Somebody had a baby or was going to have a baby and I was trying in my little child's mind to reason why it was that not everybody had babies, just women who were married. This was the fifties, you've got to remember, and it suddenly occurred to me that something bigger than me was in charge of that. God had women have babies when they were ready to. I lived with that finite understanding of the "birds and bees" for a long time before my curiosity got raised again.

I remember when we moved to Birmingham there was a big snowstorm. I don't know if I had ever seen that much snow. Maybe I had, but how we loved the fluffy white stuff. We made angels, and tunnels, and had snowball fights.

I remember storms. One day Mom and I were sitting in a rocking chair during a very bad lightning storm. Mom was singing "Rocky the Horsey" and that's when she taught me to count between the flashes of lightning and the roar of the thunder. I've never been afraid of thunder since, or lightning. I always count. How many beats tell me how far away it is.

There are so many good things about growing up. I remember standing in the backyard watching Daddy build the guinea pig cages.

Mom created the safeguard of having us put the guinea pigs under bushel baskets when we took them out of their cage. When our pets were ready to go back inside, there would be a circle where the guinea pigs had eaten the grass.

When we lived in Birmingham, Virginia and I went off to a neighbor's house. She had wonderful hard candies and we were there a long time, or it seemed like a long time to us. When we got home, Mom asked us where we had been. We were embarrassed because we didn't want her to know we had been getting candy from the neighbors, but somehow the story all came out.

I remember late nights where Virginia would hang over the sides of the bunk beds and tell me secrets. To know secrets that SHE knew always made me feel so important.

I remember David and I taking walks and all the fun things we did together – like riding our bikes. I especially liked to ride downhill. That was the most fun. All of these things are good memories.

Even though I've had trials and tribulations in my life, I've had an incredible amount of love. I've had friends who sacrificed far beyond – above and beyond – any concept of friendship I had ever known.

I have known in my days here on this earth, that there is life after this – that I'm going on to something else. I have no doubt about that whatsoever. And I'm at peace. Of course, I've had a long time to get ready to leave this show. Even though there are so many things I will miss here, I keep hoping I'll still have them in the next realm. So many messages I'm carrying to loved ones. I hope I haven't forgotten anyone. People have always been important to me. I think I've learned that from Mom and Dad.

When I was little and we had just discovered I had a hearing problem, Mom would take me to the doctor. When my hearing was tested, the nurse would give me a coupon which entitled me to an ice-cream cone. Any flavor I wanted from the downstairs drugstore. Of course, being a little child, I wanted to go right down there and get my ice cream – that minute. But Mom taught me a lesson. She said, "No, we can save your coupons. When you have three, you, your brother, and your sister can all get an ice-cream cone. It was very hard for me to do – be patient and wait, but somehow or *other, she manipulated me to do that. When the time came that I had three coupons and we were all three able to get a chocolate ice-cream cone – I know I got CHOCOLATE – I was so proud to be able to share with Virginia and David. The concept of thinking about others and looking ahead to what you can do for others was instilled in me. And that is something that has stayed with me all my life.*

Well, I've really cared about what other people were going through and I think I've been able to empathize with people. I think that's part of the reason I chose nursing as a profession. I wanted to be somewhere where I could make a difference.

It is always hard to say good-bye, but know I have loved you all and that if there is any way I can continue to be a part of your lives, I'll do it. But if not, then I'll see you on the other side.

Luke is given a gift as he retires as the Executive Vice-President of the Radio and Television Commission.

Christmas 1956 – Virginia, David and Lydia pose for a Christmas picture.

Joyce tours Bryan's House in Dallas, Texas – the home that was Lydia's dream.

37

Matt reads a book to his great grandmother, Bessie Campbell Smith at her home in Chattanooga, Tennessee.

Before you start the washing machine, always look in the pocket of Matt's jeans for his favorite picture of his mom.

Luke in his home office at 207 East Mulberry, San Antonio in 1988.

In July 1991, Scott, Lydia and Matt Allen join Joyce in the parlor of First Baptist Church of San Antonio.

PART II:
How Long, Oh Lord?

Mighty tides about me sweep,
Perils lurk within the deep,
Angry clouds o'er shade the sky,
And the tempest rises high,
Still I stand the tempest's shock,
For my anchor grips the rock.

"MY ANCHOR HOLDS"
by W. C. Martin and D.B. Towner

CHAPTER EIGHT

Matt

The ritual of his mom's birthday helps Matt prepare for his own death.

* * *

Summer 1995

When my twelve-year-old grandson Matt invited me to commemorate his mom's forty-second birthday, I wondered what he had planned. Long before her death at age thirty-nine, Lydia learned the healing value of rituals. Matt helped plant a tree on the anniversary of Bryan's death. He released balloons, wrote notes – anything that would bring comfort. Matt observed and learned from Scott and Lydia. Now, with his dad's help, he planned some rituals to celebrate his mom's birthday. So on June 21, 1995, my son David, his friend, and I drove from San Antonio to Dallas to join in Matt's tribute.

Matt's best friend Zach and his family arrived with a birthday cake. White letters on chocolate frosting read, "Happy Birthday, Lydia. We miss you." Under the lettering were three jumping dolphins. Zach's family knew dolphins were Lydia's special way to say to Matt, "I love you." After pizza, Coke, and cake, Matt announced the program.

"We will watch some videos, share memories of Mama, and then release balloons."

He clicked the remote control. The first video showed a roly-poly

Matt in the park with his mama. Matt climbed to the top of the slide, looked to see who was watching, and announced loudly, "I'm not a'scared." Everyone laughed.

The next video was a professionally made film of Bryan's House, a home for children with HIV and AIDS. This home was the fulfillment of Lydia's dream and named for her second son, Bryan.

Matt, weakened and in the end-stage of AIDS, needed to rest on the couch.

"Tell me what you remember about Mama," Matt said as he looked at me. A scene immediately came to mind.

"When Lydia was twelve, her French braids had grown so long she could sit on them. The day she had her braids cut, she had misgivings about her new look."

Tears filled our eyes as others shared memories of fun times with Lydia. Matt's mama had certainly taught him how to give a party.

A last video showed Lydia reading Matt's favorite stories, *The Giving Tree* and *The Little Prince*, and then her reminder, " Remember my love when you look at the dolphins."

I was prepared to read the book Lydia had written for Matt, *I Miss My Little Brother*. I sat beside Matt on the couch. He held the book, turned to the first page, and began to read. He hesitated at the line, "I can do for others what I could have done for Bryan," but in a weak and strained voice, he continued.

While he read, scenes from Lydia's last month flooded my mind. I recalled how she sat propped up in bed, her lists in her hands, as she courageously faced her approaching death. She wrote poetry to her friends, books for Matt, and notes of encouragement to family and friends. I watched and grieved. In spite of her pain and failing eyesight, Lydia had goals. She was determined to function until she could check the last item off her list.

My thoughts were forced back into the room when Matt finished his reading. He struggled to get up from the couch and brought a bouquet of balloons from his bedroom.

"You all choose a color, but I want the purple one. It was Mama's favorite color, and it's mine, too."

All of us walked outside. Matt needed his wheelchair. He gave each of us a balloon. One by one we let them go. A dozen balloons! The colors brilliant against a cloudless sky.

The air currents moved the colored specks. They looked like a fan across the horizon. Then the specks began to move, to shift, to realign. In a moment David shouted, "Look, the balloons have made a perfect letter L!"

"L" for Lydia? "L" for Luke?

In amazement, I stared. Was I dreaming? Did the others feel what I felt? A presence? An affirmation? Yes, I felt a PEACE I had not known since death had taken over my life.

As quickly as the letter "L" appeared, it vanished. A glorious conclusion for a birthday celebration.

Aftermath of a Storm

When a loved one dies,

Grief descends like a thunderstorm.
Pain rumbles in the distance.
Lightning forecasts the coming storm.
As the tempest nears, conflicting emotion intensifies
 and swirls into a maelstrom of grief.

Finally, the storm breaks – thoughts, emotions,
 regrets – pelt like stinging hail.
Day after day darkness obscures the light
Unceasing tears flow like rain.

Spent and exhausted, the sky rests.
Shafts of light pierce the dark canopy.
Slowly, Light reclaims soul and body.
The world clears,

The mind illuminates,
The heart warms
With the understanding
*   that after storms*
*   there is life*
*   there is growth*
*   there is love.*

– JOYCE WILLIAMS / GWEN KEPLEY

*   *   *

A Special Friendship

A young girl with compassion touches the life of a dying boy.

December 1995

Dear Natasha,

Several weeks ago I returned from Dallas. As you know, I was there to attend the memorial service for Matt. Today, as I was putting some papers in a scrapbook, my thoughts turned to you. I've enclosed a copy of the memorial service for Matt, which was held in the Dallas Horticulture Center at Fair Park .

I remember how much you two enjoyed knowing each other. When Matt and I were invited to your ranch, you taught him to ride four-wheelers. I never saw Matt happier than when he was roaring off over the trails, often waving, then circling back to where we waited.

Later that year, on Labor Day, your family invited Matt and me to your vacation home in Horseshoe Bay. You two played on the little sand beach. I knew that Matt was very ill and his days were limited, but you treated him as being very normal. Only a few of his friends gave him that gift. Many were afraid of his illness. So, I want to thank you for seeing that

Matt had some special, wonderfully exciting experiences.

This Christmas season, I am missing Matt terribly. Then I remind myself that this is his first Christmas in heaven with his mom, his little brother, Bryan, and his Daddy Luke. They must be having a great time taking walks on those golden streets.

One day, probably many years from now, maybe Matt can show you some of his discoveries. Thanks for being you – a compassionate, loving friend!

Matt's Grammy

CHAPTER NINE
Healers

Good Samaritans help me begin to heal physically and emotionally

* * *

What happens to a person who has lost so many members of her family and with each death has put their grief "on hold?" In my case, I looked brave, shed no public tears, and was constantly told how strong I was. However, inside I was carrying an explosive load of grief. When headaches became unbearable, I checked with my internist.

"No wonder you have headaches," he said. "I want you to see a physical therapist TODAY."

So began a long process. I lay on the physical therapy table day after day. She applied heat packs to my back and neck, followed by ice. Her fingers sought out the trigger points, and she literally pulled away the muscles, which she said had "frozen to the rib cage." Often I spent an hour on the table with tears flowing. Not only from the physical pain but also from the emotional – for the therapist gently probed the reasons for my "freezing."

* * *

I'm in the living room of my home. I'm clinging to the rotating ceiling fan – holding on by my fingertips. The

*fan goes faster and faster and my body swings wide over
the furniture. Fear fills every cell. My fingertips become
sweaty. I'm losing my grip.*

I awoke in a panic from this terrifying dream. My breath was
coming in short puffs. My hands were icy and shivers ran up my back.
For weeks my world had been closing in. The tasks of daily living left
me in pain. AIDS invaded my family, then Luke's sudden death. I was
barely coping. I began a study of dreams. The arguments were powerful, but I was not convinced that my subconscious could give me
insight and information in the form of a dream.

At this minute I began to question my conclusions. *Are dreams our
most underutilized resource? Am I out of touch with my inner life because
I haven't made room for dreams? Maybe Carl Jung is right. If I study this
dream – turn it over and over – what will it say to me? Is this a warning?*

I sit trembling in the dark; find my pencil and begin to record my
dream.

Even as I write, I begin to analyze. My world is chaotic. I have kept
too much pain inside. At this point I'm slipping – dangerously close to
"losing it." An inner urging says Find some help! I search my mind for
any other interpretation, but there is none. *Where will I find the energy
to seek out a new counselor?* The thought was discouraging! Twice
before I had sought counseling. Both times I had been disappointed. I
recalled the experiences well.

"Mrs. Williams, why you are seeking my help?" the first psycholo-
gist asked.

"Well, I had a frightening dream and I'm finding it hard to deal
with my family situation."

"Tell me more about your dream and your family," he said.

For the next forty minutes I briefly explained the problems since
the AIDS notification on September 17, 1985. I explained my ninety-
year-old mother's declining health and my physical problems. The
therapist listened. For weeks he listened. Finally one day he said, "This
is a very complicated situation, isn't it?" I wanted to shout, "I knew that

when I came in here! What I need is guidance – someone to help me get through this! Before I come apart at the seams!" But my introverted personality only allowed me to nod and silently shed tears.

For weeks I kept my appointment, rehearsed recent developments, resisted suggestions, wrote my check, and left. I decided not to return.

Months later, feeling desperate, I confided a small portion of my story to my pastor. He recommended a female therapist. Maybe this was the answer. Maybe I could identify better with a woman. So, again, I kept my weekly appointments and rehearsed the problems of secrecy and isolation that I faced daily. Nothing in my life seemed to make sense. I went to work, somehow got through the day, went home, ate, and went to bed. After six months, I again canceled my appointments. But I struggled daily with the shadow of death and a question which haunted me. "Would it be easier for Lydia to watch Matt die or for Matt to watch Lydia die?" If only the question would go away! But it didn't. And it wasn't mine to answer.

* * *

One day I was talking with my dear friend, Frances Mahanay. For years Frances and I had been friends. It began when our husbands served together on the staff at First Baptist Church. Both of us were teachers, and from our first meeting there was instant rapport. Frances taught at Saint Mary's Hall and introduced me to the staff there. That introduction led to my becoming employed in the Montessori School as an assistant, then a lead teacher. In 1978 I became head of the Montessori School and remained in that position until 1993.

Frances was the one friend who stayed close to me week after week, even when I was in the depths of despair. A fantastic hostess, Frances and her husband, Bill, loved to have friends for dinner. One day when Frances and I talked, she described a dinner party she and Bill had given the previous evening. She was impressed with her guests, a new chaplain and his wife who had recently joined the staff at Baptist Memorial Hospital. During the evening Frances discovered this chaplain had special training in grief counseling.

A ray of hope when I desperately needed one.

"Do you think he would see me?"

"Don't know, but I'll certainly find out."

So began a new relationship with this pastoral counselor – one that probably saved my life. For more than three years we met weekly. With his help I began to deal with and salvage the wreckage of my life – the secret areas I so carefully guarded. From our first interview, I felt Dr. Anderson could help me find my way out of the valley of the shadow of death.

* * *

Going to counseling was hard work for me. Some weeks I left the counselor's office resisting what I knew I needed to do – but was unable to attack. He urged me to look at my present circumstances, my early childhood, and my stubborn reserve and challenged me to examine my unrealistic need for privacy. Some weeks I cried all the way home. Others, I sensed a slight movement forward.

Even now when I reflect on our sessions, I'm amazed at my counselor's patience. That he could tolerate my being "stuck" week after week is still hard to believe.[2] But he was willing to walk with me through raging waters. When Matt died, he drove two hundred and fifty miles to attend his memorial service, and he stood by my side and gave me the support I needed.

After about a year of our sessions, Dr. Anderson invited me to share my story with a group of nurses at Baptist Hospital. Then he encouraged me to enroll in the Clinical Pastoral Education program for chaplains. He assured me there was healing for me and help for others when I was willing to share my story. I believed my valued friend.

50

CHAPTER TEN
Goodbye, My Love

More than two years after Luke's heart attack, I'm finally ready to tell him of my pain – to say goodbye.

* * *

Intellectually, I knew Luke was not coming back, but my need was so great! I refused to let him go. I needed his support. The day finally arrived when I knew I could begin to release him. It was time to write my letter.

Dear Luke,

Yesterday I went to visit Bill and Phyllis Nichols. Bill finished your portrait, which is to hang in the foyer dedicated to you at Woodland Baptist Church. The picture is a very good likeness. Today, I have hung your portrait over the desk where you spent so many hours. In the room where I often came and talked while you made your lists, balanced our checkbooks, or read the newspaper. I am having mixed reactions about seeing you with me so clearly again. The old longing for you to hold me in your arms, tell me you love me, and snuggle in our bed has been so real to me today. Recently I have been depressed; some days I don't get dressed. Today I didn't leave the house.

Despite my counselor's repeated suggestion, I haven't been able to tell you good-bye. The forty-four years we spent together were the happiest, and saddest, of my life. From the time we met I was fascinated by your good looks, your sense of humor, and your intelligence. It was so difficult to believe you could really be interested in me – someone who had never dated much, was basically shy, and had so little experience with the male world. Remember? Four sisters, but no brothers.

On a rainy Sunday afternoon in Harrison Bay State Park outside Chattanooga, in your old '41 Plymouth, you told me how miserable you were knowing I had dated someone else the night before. That scene remains vivid in my memory. Although I was very much attracted to you and certainly interested in developing our relationship, I don't think I had actually identified the feeling as "love." When you told me you loved me and wanted to marry me, I was speechless.

As we continued to date and I'd go with you to Signal Mountain to carry your six hundred newspapers, our relationship continued to develop. The physical attraction was ever-present. But I did come to you on June 15, 1947 as a bride proud to wear white.

Luke, today I thought about the difficult times of my pregnancy with our son, David – the hepatitis and the flight from Ft. Worth to Chattanooga. How thrilled Virginia and I were when you came to Chattanooga to take us home to Texas. The weeks we were separated were tough for me – and I'm sure for you, a struggling seminary student. But you projected a strong image, assuring me I was going to get well in spite of what the doctors and all our friends thought.

I also remembered Lydia's difficult birth, her loss of hearing in one ear, her ruptured ovary at age twelve and the snake she found on the bank of the San Antonio river and invited to live under her bed. Wouldn't you love to know how long that snake roamed our house and how he finally escaped?

This week a five-year-old student at Saint Mary's Hall was killed when her bike was hit by a car. As a result, the pain associated with your sudden death, Lydia's death, and even Bryan's death came flooding back. I haven't been willing to come to terms with losing you at a time in our lives when we were probably sharing, supporting, and loving each other as never before.

I've said to many people that when you became the executive vice president of the Radio and Television Commission the complexion of our marriage changed. The time we had together was quality time and I loved it. I loved sitting with you on the back pew of First Baptist Church. I can almost sense your arm around me, making me feel loved and wanted.

When you were involved in the various churches we served, I sometimes felt neglected. But in those seven years we commuted between San Antonio and Fort Worth, we grew in our respect for each other and valued our gifts – especially after we got the news about AIDS.

* * *

People have said to me that the loss of a child is the most difficult loss a person can experience. Maybe that is true for some, but not for me. Luke, you were my best friend, my soul mate for forty-four years.

How I have survived these months, I'm not sure. I grappled with my doubt and wondered if God cared, and some days I was certain he didn't. I had the support of family, friends, and my counselor. I buried myself in the work at Saint Mary's Hall.

I think I'm saying all this to explain to myself why it has been almost two years and I still haven't been able to say good-bye. I know you are dead! I hate it that you are dead! I hate it that we will never build our retirement home in Georgia on Chickamauga Creek, or travel in our trailer and enjoy a slower pace of life TOGETHER. I hate being alone. I want to hear your key in the door, have you kneel by my chair and snuggle into my neck. I hate the empty place in our bed – a very present reminder you aren't coming back. OH, how it hurts!

I know if I'm to heal physically and emotionally I must go on with life. I want the years remaining to count for something. The bereavement workshop in Phoenix opened my eyes to some new possibilities. And the "Life After Loss" support group I'm leading at Woodland is apparently meeting needs. In preparation for the sessions, I'm having to examine my *own needs – those of facing the future without you, Bryan, or Lydia. Also, Mom and Matt's declining health is a constant worry.*

Luke, some day I want to go back to Rockport and walk around the bay, look at the water, smell the salt air, and remember those final happy days we spent in the condo. How glad I am we didn't know you would be leaving me so soon. So many beautiful memories...I am sure we would have purchased that condo had you lived, but I'm thankful I realized I couldn't proceed with it alone.

* * *

It is dusk and you are looking down at me from the portrait on the wall. Even now, I'm so full of love for you. Our years together are sealed in my heart forever. I know you wouldn't want me to shrivel up and die – but to move on, make the years ahead count. So this letter is my good-bye. For the dreams that died with you, I grieve. I'm grateful to have come into your life and grown with you, to see you become a person loved and respected by everyone who knew you.

I was, and am, so proud of your accomplishments. You were a great granddad. I regret we only got to take two of our grandchildren for their week in New York City.

After writing this, as a part of my good-bye, I watched the video of your memorial service and the one of Lydia's. Now I can put the tapes away.

Goodbye, my love,

Joyce

In the last months of his life, Matt comes to San Antonio. As he gets off the plane, before saying "hello," he announces, "Grammy, I've got a question. When I come to San Antonio do you think a lot about my mom?" To my nod, he responded, " Well I do, too, so it is kinda hard to come here."

Matt - what a smile!

Lydia decides to cut her braids. The beautician snips them just below the ear lobe. At home, we carefully line a box with tissue and pack the braids away. Today, they remain in my memory box.

A children's book, I REMEMBER MAMA, tells the story of Matt's celebration of his mom's birthday following her death. The released balloons fan out, then realign to form the letter "L" Happy Birthday, Mama.

The Woodland Baptist Church is located at 15315 Huebner Road in San Antonio. Joyce is a charter member.

PART III:

Moving into the Light

Troubles almost whelm the soul
Griefs like billows o're me roll,
Tempters seek to lure astray,
Storms obscure the light of day;
But in Christ I can be bold,
I've an anchor that shall hold.

"MY ANCHOR HOLDS"
by W. C. Martin and D.B. Towner

CHAPTER ELEVEN
Work

Overwhelmed by losses, I look for ways to keep functioning.

* * *

I was still trying to bring some sense to my life. Most days I functioned fairly well. After retirement in 1993, I decided to go back to
school for additional training in grief counseling and pastoral care.
After I was certified as a bereavement facilitator by the American
Academy of Bereavement, I volunteered as a pediatric chaplain with
seriously ill and terminally ill patients and their parents.

As my friends asked me what I was doing, I explained the work of
a chaplain. Then I would brace myself for their response.

"Joyce, when you have had so much death in your family, why
would you open yourself to all that additional pain?"

Some days I asked myself that question – especially when I stood
beside parents as they watched their child's life ebb away. In pondering
my reasons for volunteering, I came to realize each of us must find our
own way to grieve. After months and months, I could now acknowl-
edge my pain – and I could open myself to the pain of others. The
process of recovery began.

I struggled with a decision about enrolling in another unit of
Clinical Pastoral Education. When I finally made the decision to enroll,
my resolution was firm. In this new group I would carefully skirt

around my grief issues. After all, I told myself, I was healing, and the new group would not need to know my entire story.

*   *   *

I arrived at the hospital for my first class in Unit Three and was invited into the chapel at Saint Luke's Hospital for a "brief ceremony" – a changing of supervisors. The retiring supervisor stood before the group. There were three women and three men ranging in age from the early thirties to me, the senior citizen.

"Before we take communion, I want to share a story with you," the supervisor announced.

In a quiet voice the chaplain began to read from *The Little Prince*. I knew the story well; it was one of Lydia's favorites. When he finished, we took communion, sang "Blest Be the Tie That Binds," and moved upstairs to our classroom.

Interested in my peers, I looked around. A strapping six-foot-tall man was wiping tears from his eyes.

"Our final song brought back memories," he explained. "When I was leaving a congregation I loved, they sang that song to me. I didn't realize the emotions were still so powerful."

"You have just experienced what we call evocative memory," explained the supervisor. "We all have it. We feel certain emotions, which often surprise us, as memories flood our minds."

It hit me like a tidal wave. Tear after tear trickled down my right cheek, then my left. I fumbled for a tissue and tried to swallow my feelings. As discreetly as possible, I brushed away the tears. I fought to suppress the grief that flowed over me in waves. The room got quiet. The group waited. I felt I had to say something, but what?

Finally able to speak, I said, " Today, I too experienced evocative memory. I was carried back to the Botanical Gardens in Dallas where I watched my daughter, Lydia, read *The Little Prince* into a camcorder. The story was recorded for her son to watch after her death. Both my daughter and my grandson are no longer living." For the next few minutes I was in my own private world of pain. So much for my decision to skim lightly over my grief issues.

* * *

The first class ended at 1:15 P.M. I was due downtown, some fifteen miles away, at 2:30 to tell my story to a group of interns studying to be chaplains. Knowing that I could not speak on an empty stomach after such an emotional morning, I pulled into the closest sandwich shop, ordered at the drive through, and parked under a tree to eat.

The activities of the morning swirled in my thoughts. "What is the likelihood of the story of *The Little Prince* being told on the one day I vowed to conceal my grief issues?" I pondered. "Not one in a million," I answered!

A voice in my head said, *So you planned to skim lightly over the grief issues? You didn't ask ME about that. The story from The Little Prince was no accident. Grief is a part of the person you are. You are sick of losses and think you are ready to leave them behind, but I have other plans for you.*

Thoughtfully, I finished my sandwich and drove into town. En route I found myself praying. *Oh, Lord, thank you for making your presence real to me today. You have seemed so far away. Thanks for reminding me that you are concerned with decisions I make – even those I hesitate to bring to you. Thanks for your patience with me in spite of my doubts. You know I am basically shy – you know I've been reluctant to tell my story; if that is what you want, you open the doors and I'll speak.*

* * *

One Sunday morning I was the on-call chaplain and needed to conduct a short devotional service for patients and hospital staff. Seven people arrived in the chapel and sat in a circle. I felt an illustration from a sermon I had heard might be helpful. The story went like this: a missionary home on furlough was showing his parents pictures of the people he served in New Guinea. One picture showed women carrying sixty-pound loads on their heads. In this area there were no bridges, so when the water wasn't deep the women waded across the streams. But New Guinea has lots of rain, and sometimes the current became especially swift. "Then," I described what the missionary had explained, "the women doubled their load to keep from losing their footing. The extra weight held them steady until they reached the other side."

I paused, then added, "Most of you carry burdens as I do. Ever wonder if God knows the amount of 'weight' you need to keep your footing through the danger spots? Have you asked for patience to carry your burden until it is safe for him to lighten your load?" Psalm 37:5 says, "Commit your way to the Lord: trust in Him."

CHAPTER TWELVE
The Fog lifts

My deep feelings are best expressed on paper.

* * *

Spring 1994

As silently as the stars appeared, the fog moved in, surrounding my small grey patio home. I watched the white fluff obliterate red velvet amaryllis, pink pots of begonias, and mounds of asparagus fern. My mind drifted back to another morning when fog enveloped the quadraplex where I lived in the Monte Vista area of San Antonio.

At that time I was employed as a school administrator at a private school, Saint Mary's Hall. Being somewhat compulsive, I was following my usual morning routine. Reluctantly, I crawled out of bed when the alarm sounded at 5:40 A.M. and peered outside to see what the day might be like.

I looked over the tops of giant trees that surrounded the spacious, second-floor apartment where I had lived for twenty years. Here – as a nature lover, bird watcher and environmentalist – I felt inspired by the world outside my walls. The woodlands beneath my window housed red squirrels, cottontail rabbits, and ringtail raccoons. Nightly a mockingbird warbled to his mate from the top of the telephone pole, and cardinals found a place to nest in rosebushes. Flickers discovered ants when they poked their beaks into the mulberry tree.

* * *

My upstairs bedroom window was a perfect frame for the slender steeple of the Trinity Baptist Church. Spotlights penetrated the night sky and highlighted the elegant lines. Shivering, I wished I were wearing a heavier nightgown, but I refused to go to the closet for my robe. I stared, deep in thought, rehearsing the schedule for the day ahead. As I meditated, the timer at the church clicked off and the illuminated steeple disappeared. I moved quickly from the window. Why bother to gaze at a black abyss?

Dressing was automatic. To save time, each night I selected, pressed, and coordinated my outfit. Now sitting at my dressing table, I applied my make-up with quick strokes then moved back to the window.

At the base of the steeple a pink glow was creeping into the eastern sky. I watched it come alive. Moment by moment, inch by inch, the outline of the steeple became distinct. Slowly the sky brightened and bathed the steeple in light. Time seemed unimportant.

In recent months San Antonio had been plagued with multiple days of fog, more than I ever remembered. Some mornings my window framed only haze, mist, and fluffy white puffs. However, on this morning the steeple had sharp distinct outlines. But as I watched, a mist rolled toward me. In seconds the steeple was completely obscured by fog. I was fascinated; I couldn't move. Soon the fog engulfed my building. I had the sensation of being smothered, closed off – lost in the mist.

A quick look at my watch told me I needed to move or I would be late for school. I collected my purse and briefcase and headed for the garage. But the "smothered feel" stayed with me. Why the impact? Was it because in the last couple of years so many experiences in my life had left me feeling alone – lost? Why did it feel like the light that illuminated my way had been shut off?

I pulled out of the driveway and in minutes stopped for a red light, then I was able to increase my speed. Since I had traveled the same route to school for almost twenty years, driving was somewhat automatic, which gave me the opportunity to ponder my early morning experience. In my mind's eye I could reconstruct the steeple; I knew it well.

Within minutes I arrived at school, pulled into my parking space and dropped my head. Show me, Lord. Teach me. Help me understand.

With head bowed and eyes closed, I thought about the steeple – its brilliance in the spotlights, glorious in the pink eastern sky, or slipping into total darkness. Without an audible word, I knew. The steeple was solid, secure – an anchor – even if I could not see it.

Thank you, Lord, for your presence
  – for the ability to walk by faith, not by sight
  – for the assurance that the sun will rise again and silhouette
    the steeple
  – for hope that comes with each new day.

* * *

Churches are a vital part of my past, present, and future. Churches have always been important in my life, and steeples have held a special fascination. As a young child I watched the Spring Creek Baptist Church burn, terrified as the ancient wooden structure was consumed like a haystack. When the flames reached the steeple, a hole opened around the base and the steeple toppled to the ground. Only the brass bell survived.

* * *

As a teenager living in Tennessee, my social activities were church-centered. As an adult, churches in Texas offered me avenues of service and challenged me to spiritual growth.

Now, as an "experienced adult," I belong to a young church – the Woodland Baptist congregation. I knew of its possible existence before the church was organized. A group from Ridgewood Mission, sponsored by First Baptist of San Antonio, and a group from Manor Baptist, who owned property on Huebner Road, were meeting to see if the two groups might merge. Luke met with both groups and dreamed of the possibility that the two groups might form one strong church. He declared it a miracle when the two groups agreed and formed Woodland.

Following Luke's death, I faced a difficult decision. Return to my many friends at First Baptist or become a part of the Woodland congregation? This small group met in a rented glass factory while raising money to build a building. Always before I had attended the church of my parent's choice or one where Luke served as minister of music, education, or administration, sometimes all three. With ambivalent feelings, I decided to join hands with the Woodland congregation.

Throughout our married lives, Luke and I had tithed our income to the church where we served and held membership. Now I faced another decision I would have to make without Luke's help. Did I need to contribute the tithe of his estate? If so, to what cause?

* * *

On October 6, 1991, the foyer of the new sanctuary at Woodland was dedicated to Luke in appreciation of his services as volunteer minister of education. The plaque under his portrait reads:

"'Behold, I will do a new thing.' Isaiah 43:19

He envisioned the 'new thing' and helped make it happen."

Aware of the time and energy Luke had devoted to Woodland – and of his love of music – a piano, choir robes, and music folders were contributed in his honor. All were in place the day the new sanctuary was dedicated. My dream for a future building at Woodland is a steeple.

* * *

To this day, steeples continue to fascinate me. A tall white spire in Dallas haunts my memory. In the hysteria of the Ryan White era, the Wilshire Baptist Church quietly reached out to Lydia, Scott, Matthew, and Bryan. Although the church body did not extend an invitation to this troubled family to attend their services, the pastor, Dr. Bruce McIver, and individual members quietly sought ways to support.

When my daughter and son-in-law feared eviction from rented quarters they longed to buy a home, but medical expenses consumed most of their resources. Members of the Wilshire congregation generously contributed to the down payment on a small cottage near White Rock Lake – it was a home from which they could not be evicted.

One Saturday morning a group of men from the Wilshire church drove trucks and trailers to Ft. Worth and moved the family's belongings to Dallas to the new home. At lunchtime the men brought in brightly colored coolers filled with sandwiches, cookies, and cold drinks – a picnic to share with the family.

Many acts of kindness followed. One day when I was in Dallas, the doorbell rang. As I opened the door, the smell of freshly baked bread filled the air. The beautiful lady holding the loaves identified herself as a member of the Wilshire congregation.

So support came often and in many forms. A "missionary house" owned and furnished by Wilshire Baptist was made available whenever our family needed a place of respite. On our last visit to Dallas before Matt's death, my son David and I often retreated to the sanctuary of this house, and we were very thankful.

CHAPTER THIRTEEN
A Final Visit to Dallas

David and I drove to Dallas. Matt had called.

* * *

"Uncle David, I just need to tell you that I'm going to die."

"Matt, I'm sorry, I don't know what to say."

"That's okay, Uncle David, no one knows what to say, or what to do."

As our last visit to Matt began, the hospice nurse arrived.

"Come to the bedroom," she said, "this is going to take a while. You can visit with Matt while I work."

David and I followed her to Matt's bed. At this point Matt weighed only forty pounds. Seeing him in his emaciated condition was so painful for me that I could only stay in the room a few minutes at a time. The nurse applied padded bandages to Matt's knees, elbows, wrists – any area where the bone structure was pushing through the skin.

I watched in amazement as Matt tolerated the change of dressings. He would close his eyes, breath deeply, and then try to smile.

"Grammy, I'm so tired!"

What I wouldn't have given to take Matt in my arms and rock him to sleep, but any touch was painful. I stayed in the bedroom a few minutes, then retreated to the kitchen and sobbed. When I could control my tears, I slipped back into the bedroom.

* * *

For months Scott had lovingly cared for Matt day and night, and with hospice help, Matt was kept as comfortable as possible. From June to November, Matt's condition steadily worsened. On October 4, 1995, Matt turned thirteen and reached his goal of being a teenager. During a windstorm on November 10, his spirit left his stricken body.

CHAPTER FOURTEEN

To My Woodland Church Family

January 11, 1996

Dear Woodland Family,

On November 10, 1995, my grandson Matt Allen died. He had been in hospice care since September 1994. His name appeared on and off our prayer list as his condition deteriorated.

Even as death approached, Matt was successful in many areas. He lived to see his thirteenth birthday in spite of being infected with the HIV virus during a blood transfusion before his birth.

So Matt's death, Bryan's death, and Lydia's death bring closure to eleven years of my dealing with the reality of AIDS. Regardless of how the disease is contracted, it is devastating to a family. You, my church family, have been supportive in so many, many ways. Often my emotions were so raw that I was not able to respond appropriately to your words of encouragement, but I heard them! During the recent holiday season I have been reclaiming my memories, occasions that are forever engraved in my mind. Above my desk, beautifully done in counted cross-stitch, is a saying which reads:

Some people come into our lives and quietly go.
Others stay for awhile and leave footprints
on our hearts and we are never the same.

Thanks to each of you for your footprints!

CHAPTER FIFTEEN
Cadence of My Heart

I regain a sense of balance when I feel God's presence.

* * *

Summer 1998

My friend Carol from my writers' critique group and I had come a second time to the Yellowstone Institute to a nature writing workshop.

Thunder rolled overhead. The smell of sulphur drifted through this area of the park. I was only vaguely aware of other group members in the distance. I took a seat on a fallen log.

My hunger had been satisfied with a picnic lunch. I sat motionless and watched billows of steam float heavenward. The rhythmic beat of the bubbling pools, called paint pots, echoed like the cadence of my heart. I struggled to concentrate on the handiwork of God around me, but my thoughts strayed. I was still trying to resolve my grief issues. I wanted desperately to find peace, relief from pain that began so many years earlier.

"*MOM*," the hysterical voice of my younger daughter began, "*I've just had a call from the blood bank in San Francisco....*" One by one they had slipped away from me. In my mind's eye, I can see the ashes of the three stricken with AIDS, scattered in the Pacific at Half Moon Bay.

I struggled to think clearly as I opened the small notebook to record the wonders of God's creation surrounding me.

Suddenly, a tiny black spider appeared on my page and marched back and forth.

Sitting on the edge of my notebook, he peered at the written words. The spider, no bigger than a pencil lead, left my notebook and marched across my fingers. He examined each wrinkle and vein, then moved on.

Underfoot, delicate spruce cones carpeted the ground as far as I could see; their fragrance was overpowered by the scent of sulphur. Among the spruce were lodge-pole pine and Douglas fir. Some were only three inches tall, and others soared to touch foamy white clouds interspersed with thunderheads. I rose to follow a long, narrow path bordered with goldenrod and purple thistle. Dandelion puffs blew in the breeze. Short stalks of rough milkweed pods burst open. Air currents carried clouds of seed propelled by tufts of silken hair. Shadows of giant Douglas fir trees fell across the narrow path.

Behind me, a beetle sang his "click, click, click" song, the rhythmic beat distinctive above the cadence of the paint pots. I moved from the shadows into the sunlight and brushed away a mosquito buzzing around my head. I glanced at the growing thunderheads. Did they reach to heaven? Could they reach Luke? Could he know where I was and how much I missed him? I recalled his touch on my shoulder at midnight and the panic in his voice as if it were yesterday. *"Honey, get up and dress quickly. I need to go to the hospital."* Fourteen hours later, Luke, my beloved companion of forty-four years, was dead.

I looked down, trying to thrust these thoughts from my mind. At my feet, I spied an object – a rock? No – a fossil of the Permian period encapsulating minute sea animals.

The sound of the gurgling paint pots drew me closer to the sulphur-laden pond, but I could not abandon my interest in the fossil formation. Why was it here? Was it lost? As lost as I'd felt for many of these torturous years? But there was another, larger fossil. I turned it over with the toe of my shoe. Underneath, curled into a perfect circle, was a shiny, bronze-colored worm. I stopped to record my findings, looked back, and he was gone. GONE! One minute he was here, the next he was gone. Just like the people I loved. My husband, my daughter, my two grandsons, and my mom. I had also recently lost a friend.

I recalled the newscaster's recent words, which were imprinted on my mind. *"An eighty-nine-year-old resident of an upscale nursing home was murdered Monday evening. A suspect is being sought by police."* What kind of person could smother a kind, elderly woman and then choke her? Then a picture flashed on the TV screen – it was my friend of twenty years. Since her stroke four months earlier, I had visited her daily, washed her gowns, and delivered her mail. I did for her the things I could not do for my mother in her last illness because she was far away.

Just when I felt I was healing from my previous losses, my friend's violent death caused my accumulated grief to erupt once more. Had several years of work by doctors, physical therapists, and my pastoral counselor been wiped out by the murder of my beloved friend? Thoughts, emotions, and regrets stung me like hail. Could I survive this latest loss?

Moving on around the pond, a white butterfly flitted across the path. The sun was shining, but I felt a drop of rain on my nose. The clouds overhead darkened. So did my spirits. All around me stood tall, magnificent trees, but in front of me on the path an uprooted tree jutted from the ground. Another death. *Why did this tree fall into the steaming water? Was it felled in a storm? Diseased? Or did man destroy it?*

* * *

I reviewed the list in my notebook. The spider, small as a pencil lead, towering thunderheads, smelly paint pots – all were woven into the Creator's plan, which at this moment was a puzzle to me. Pain racked my body.

Finally, I followed the path that encircled the gigantic bubbling pond into a more isolated area. Another log invited me to meditate. Sunshine warmed the tight muscles in my back and soon I felt sleepy.

A chattering squirrel caused me to look up. *How long have I been here?* Have I been dreaming? I again opened my notebook . A voice, not audible, said, *Look behind you!* Still half awake, I turned. In a cove beside the path, sunlight streamed into a crystal cave. The slow drip, drip, drip of mineral-laden water had formed stalagmites which resembled the pipes of a meticulously crafted organ. From my seat on the log, I was transported to a cathedral built one drop at a time. My sad heart fluttered – then filled with gratitude.

Gazing at this glorious sight, I knew this cathedral was no accident. It had been prepared for me. God did care. He had not forsaken me. He had come searching for me and waited patiently for me to feel his presence. Now, I was confident I could heal, one moment at a time.

The rhythmic beat of the bubbling paint pots echoed the cadence of my heart as it sang, "MY GOD, HOW GREAT THOU ART! HOW GREAT THOU ART!"

CHAPTER SIXTEEN
Life Ahead

On my life's scale, losses are balanced with memories.

* * *

Spring 1999

As a senior citizen I have the advantage of reflecting on seven decades. Some days I sit in my easy chair and think of the year when I was nine. One Saturday my mom washed and ironed the best dress each of my sisters owned in preparation for going "downtown" to the Ridgedale Baptist Church for Sunday School. She washed our hair – my older sister first, then mine, my sister Gloria, and Baby Nan. Shoe polishing came next. Finally, Mom baked a cake and got chicken ready to fry for Sunday dinner.

The Ridgedale Church was very different from the small one-room church I had known as a four – or five-year-old-the one I watched burn. Ridgedale was a yellow brick building with a tall steeple and high steps leading up to the entrance. In my mind's eye I can still climb those steps, walk quietly into the stately sanctuary, and seat myself on the right side of the pulpit. I can almost see my dad in the bass section of the choir and more important, remember that he could see me. In this church I did my first public speaking. The pastor's wife asked me to recite the "love chapter" from First Corinthians. I rehearsed all week and at the appointed time repeated the whole chapter without a flaw.

Today passages from the Bible still sustain me. In leading a support group, I found Isaiah 49:14-16 (the Amplified Bible).

> *"But Zion said, 'The Lord has forsaken me, and my Lord has forgotten me.' (And the Lord answered) 'Can a woman forget her nursing child, that she should not have compassion on the son of her womb? Yes, they may forget, yet I will not forget you. Behold I have indelibly imprinted (tattooed) a picture of you on each of the palms of my hands.'"*

Desperately looking for ways to make sense of my pain, several years ago I began to look for people who needed someone to walk beside them through their dark valleys. An opportunity opened for me to serve as a volunteer pediatric chaplain at Methodist Hospital. I spent Thursday afternoons in the pediatric intensive care unit with parents who had seriously ill or terminally ill children. On Tuesday evenings I sponsored a sing-along in the playroom for children who had their doctors' permission to leave their rooms. I especially encouraged brothers and sisters, even cousins who visited the patients, to sing with us. One of my major concerns, and often that of parents, was the impact a serious illness of a family member had on the siblings.

If it is true that one child of every seven will experience the death of a parent, brother, or sister by the age of ten, I wondered, *How can I help?* In early 1999 I investigated a new work, the Children's Bereavement Center of South Texas. I was drawn to the idea of helping children heal after a death. I took twenty-five hours of training to become a group facilitator. A few weeks later I agreed to become the volunteer program coordinator. For me, the time I spend with grieving children is healing.

* * *

Today, in the process of healing, my life is no longer on hold. Writing has given me the opportunity to share my thoughts about the years of struggle with death and dying and the grief I experienced. From the time of Bryan's death in 1987, I have changed. I'm not the same person who buried my husband Luke in 1991, my daughter Lydia in 1992, my mother Bessie in 1994, and my second grandson Matt in 1995.

Writing this memoir – bringing my feelings to the surface – has facilitated my healing, and my prayer is that you, too, will heal as you walk with me out of my darkness into the light.

As I began collecting the material for this book, the word "serendipity" faced me repeatedly. In looking through my files, I would unexpectedly find a letter, a poem, or a verse of scripture that I wanted to include. Perhaps the most significant serendipity came when I found an audiocassette Lydia prepared for me, her brother, and her sister, just days before she died. Several years after her death, I was looking for a tape to take to the sing-along at Methodist Hospital. I picked up one I did not recognize. I have no memory of receiving the tape or adding it to my collection. I slid the cassette into the recorder and immediately recognized my daughter's voice. What does that verse in Hebrews say? "(S)he being dead, yet speaketh."

I have been asked many times, "How do you handle all your pain?" I don't have "pat" answers. There have been times when I could find no comfort anywhere! I was angry with God. I had trouble praying or reading the Bible. From early childhood I had been taught to fear God. I had no idea that doubt and faith could exist side by side.

I know now that although it brought me little comfort, it was important for me to meet with Christian friends for worship. Music of all kinds, but especially the old hymns, kept my heart from hardening in the worst of the storms.

I am also grateful to my writing critique group and the South Texas Chapter of the Society for Children's Book Writers and Illustrators. I have lost count of the number of workshops I have attended. Recently I have edited stories Lydia wrote and stories I have written. Getting them published is a slow process, but I press on.

In the last several years there have been many opportunities to tell my story here in San Antonio and on the state and national level. Still a very private person, I consider each invitation carefully and I am grateful that my health permits me to speak.

With each birthday I seem to find more comfort and challenge in small things. For many years a gold ribbon with the words ATTITUDE IS EVERYTHING hung on Lydia's bathroom mirror. Today it is taped to mine. During my complicated grief, my attitude often slipped. However, as healing progresses, I find I have integrated the words ATTITUDE IS EVERYTHING into my life. My daughter's example propels me to reach out to people who hurt. With God's help, the support of family, church friends, and my pastoral counselor, I'm moving from darkness to light.

*   *   *

As a part of the facilitator training at the Children's Bereavement Center, each volunteer is asked to write their own obituary. *What do I want my family and friends to remember?* The words to a song sung recently by our choir clearly states my goal.

FIND US FAITHFUL

> *Oh may all who come behind us find us faithful –*
> *May the fire of our devotion light their way.*
> *May the footprints that we leave, lead them to believe*
> *And the lives we live inspire them to obey.*
> *Oh may all who come behind us find us faithful.*

– LYRICS AND MUSIC BY JON MOHR

EPILOGUE

May 2002

Recently I attended a women's retreat. Part of the day we spent in silent meditation. Then we were given an assignment: Recall and record times when you felt God's presence in your life. In completing this assignment I became acutely aware of my Christian heritage.

Dear God,

Before I entered first grade at age five, my mother taught me to sing "Jesus Loves Me," "Jesus Loves the Little Children of the World," and "Sunbeam, Sunbeam, I'll be a Sunbeam for Him." Then at nine, when I wiggled and squirmed during each worship service, especially during the invitation time, I sometimes woke my baby sister so I could take her outside and miss the invitation. You probably were smiling.

During this period I tried to avoid my Sunday School teacher who wanted to sit with me in church. But one week while Mom was sewing, she insisted that I memorize Romans 10:9-10, and soon I made a profession of faith, accepting your son as best a nine-year-old understands.

I thank you for the opportunities to grow and serve even as a teenager – directing children's Christmas programs, working in vacation Bible school, and sending newsletters to church members in uniform. And thank you for pastors, youth leaders, and other adults who encouraged my spiritual growth. Thanks especially for my cousins, Dr. and Mrs. T.B. Maston, who took me to the Ridgecrest Conference Center twice and allowed me to experience their family. I got to know Tom Mac, their son who had cerebral palsy (who was almost my same age) and who spent his entire seventy-something years in a wheelchair.

There have been many times, God, when you watched over me, loved me when I was unlovely and healed me, even when the hepatitis during my pregnancy caused me to turn green. Thank you!

Words cannot describe my gratitude for your gift of a loving, caring companion who allowed me to be a part of his service to you. You know how angry, hurt, and disillusioned I was when he was snatched away – at a time when I needed his support so desperately. I still do not understand the timing. However, I have come to accept the fact that for now I "see through a glass darkly." But I rely on your promise – that someday you will make it all plain.

Seven months after Luke's death, at the time of Lydia's death, the pain seemed unbearable, but you gently reached loving arms to me in the shape of family members, a host of friends, and a new church congregation. Also, you guided me to a therapist who has truly been a gift. Inspired books have given me knowledge and inspiration. Some have given me an escape from the pain. Thank you for the gift of sight and the ability to read.

Doors of service have opened and doors have closed. The six years as pediatric chaplain at Methodist Hospital were a growth spurt, as have been my years with the Children's Bereavement Center.

At this point I have no idea what you hold for me in the future. However, I'm willing to walk in all the light I have – then take one more scary step of faith into the darkness. I now have confidence, for you have walked with me seven times through the valley of the shadow of death. Knowing more trips into that valley face me, I rely on your rod and your staff to comfort me. My desire is to see thee more clearly, to love thee more dearly, to serve thee sincerely.

THIS IS MY PRAYER!

The Luke Williams family at Christmas time, 1953 – Virginia is four and a half, David is two and Lydia is six months.

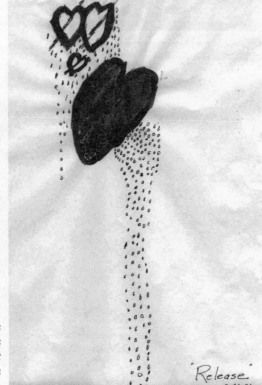

"Release"
5-20-93

Joyce turns to art to express her overwhelming sadness when a student at Saint Mary's Hall is killed in a bicycle accident.

A bronze plaque is placed in the courtyard of Saint Mary's Hall's Montessori School in 1993.

Matt's favorite shirt.

Lydia visits her grandmother in Chattanooga.

ACKNOWLEDGEMENTS

Grief, for so many years a taboo subject, can now be discussed openly. My thanks to pioneers who researched death and dying and affirm that grief follows loss. Every person suffers loss, some that is painful beyond words. However, when a dream – or our hope – falls apart, something inside us comes unglued. It hurts to let go of some-one special, but giving up a dream is sometimes our breaking point. So, as one dream dies, our search for another must begin.

I am indebted to many busy people who took time to read and re-read the early versions of the manuscript and encouraged me to keep writing. Among those are Lee Stone, Bill and Frances Mahanay, Rose Christian, Jan Lischer, Jimmy Elrod, Barbara Higdon, Dick and Doris Lee, my sisters, Nan Nave, Gloria Carowan, and Pam Boone; Phyllis Nichols, Kay Nolan, Lee Ann Rathbun, Letha Crouch, Dr. Lindell Anderson, Dr. Martha Morse, Dr. George Mason and Maria Biediger. Each provided valuable insights that are reflected in the final version of the book. Chapter 14, "Cadence of My Heart," was first published as a personal reflection in The Journal of Pastoral Care (Vol. 53, No. 3, Fall 1999, p. 359).

I am deeply grateful for the tribute to my daughter, Lydia, written and delivered by her beloved, care-giving friend, Maria Bellantoni. Each time I read the tribute I am comforted, and my heart is stirred as I recall the dignity with which she spoke at Lydia's memorial service.

Throughout their lives, a dedicated doctor tenderly cared for my two terminally ill grandsons. I thank God for Dr. Janet Squires of the Children's Medical Center in Dallas. When the fear of AIDS caused

Matt to be isolated, Dr. Squires allowed her three children to visit Matt. Often they invited him to their home. What a blessing this family has been through the years.

Triumph Over Grief, originally written as proof to myself that something positive can emerge from negative experiences, would not have been possible without the support of my family: my daughter, Virginia, her husband Dennis, and my four beautiful granddaughters; my son, David, my grandson, Brandon, my sisters, nieces and nephews, and my church family, the congregation of the Woodland Baptist Church, San Antonio, Texas.

Someone said, "Growth can emerge from the very same chaos that threatens ruin." Thanks be to God.

ABOUT THIS BOOK

Proceeds from this book will benefit Bryan's House, Lydia's House, and the Children's Bereavement Center of South Texas.

ABOUT BRYAN'S HOUSE:

Bryan's House, a licensed, nationally-acclaimed pediatric AIDS model program, was named for my grandson, Bryan Caleb Allen, the first child in Dallas County to die of AIDS. Lydia envisioned such a home when  as an AIDS educator she could find no foster care for children with AIDS and cared for three young children in her home when their own mother had to be hospitalized.

Bryan's House opened in 1987 after months of grant writing, soliciting funds, and physical labor. Lydia and her co-worker, Stephanie

Held, were able to see their dream come true. In 1994, Bryan's House was one of nineteen organizations nationwide recognized by the U.S. Department of Health and Human Services for their dedication in treatment and care of persons living with HIV and AIDS.

On May 6, 1996, a covered playground at Bryan's House was dedicated in memory of Matt Allen, Bryan's older brother, who died November 5, 1995 from complications due to AIDS.

ABOUT LYDIA'S HOUSE:

Lydia's House is modeled after Bryan's House and is named for Lydia Williams Allen, R.N., mother of Bryan and Matt. The house began as a project of Love and Action/ Southwestern Ohio and the Greater Cincinnati Christian Community. In June, 1998, the house began to serve HIV affected families.

ABOUT THE CHILDREN'S BEREAVEMENT CENTER OF SOUTH TEXAS:

Since 1997, the Center has provided a safe, supportive environment for children, adolescents, and their families to express feelings, share experiences, and grieve the death of a loved one. The goal: bring together children and adolescents with similar loss experiences to help diminish their feelings of loneliness and isolation. At the Center, children may clarify death-related issues which are confusing or frightening. In May 2000, a house at 332 West Craig in the Monte Vista

CHILDREN'S BEREAVEMENT CENTER
OF SOUTH TEXAS

section of San Antonio was purchased to enable the Center to serve more grieving families.

As program coordinator, I am involved in the training course given to new facilitators, promote and lead two six-week sessions per year for children three through five years old, and have facilitated the nine through twelve age group, which meets twice a month. Most of these youngsters have experienced the sudden death of a parent. One young boy lost both his mother and father in an automobile accident.

My training leads me to believe that children who face and deal with the death of a significant person in their life at an early age will avoid problems that often arise in adulthood when pain is ignored. When not dealt with early, pain surfaces at a later time and seriously complicates productive lives.

CHRONOLOGY
DATES IMPORTANT TO THIS STORY:

1982 Blood transfusions given to Lydia Allen in
San Francisco, California

   Birth of Matthew Benjamin Allen in San Francisco, California

1985 Birth of Bryan Caleb Allen in Colorado Springs, Colorado

1986 Death of Bryan Caleb Allen in Dallas, Texas

1987 Bryan's House opens in Dallas, Texas

1991 Death of Luke Williams in San Antonio, Texas

1992 Death of Lydia Allen in Dallas, Texas

1994 Death of Bessie C. Smith (Joyce's mother) in
Chattanooga, Tennessee

1995 Death of Matthew Benjamin Allen in Dallas, Texas

1998 Lydia's House begins operation in Cincinnati, Ohio

2000 Reivers Press of San Diego publishes
I Miss My Little Brother and *I Remember Mama*

"My Anchor Holds"

Tho' the angry surges roll
on my tempest driven soul,
I am peaceful for I know
Wildly tho' the winds may blow,
I've an anchor safe and sure
And in Christ I shall endure.

Mighty tides about me sweep,
Perils lurk within the deep,
Angry clouds o'er shade the sky,
And the tempest rises high,
Still I stand the tempest's shock,
For my anchor grips the rock.

Troubles almost whelm the soul
Griefs like billows o're me roll,
Tempters seek to lure astray,
Storms obscure the light of day;
But in Christ I can be bold,
I've an anchor that shall hold.

by W. C. Martin and D.B. Towner

END NOTES

1   The AIDS problem was so complex that we wondered if Lydia
would live to see her story in print. She suggested it be copyright-
ed in my name. However, the book was released in time for her to
personally autograph copies for her family, friends, and people
with whom she worked at Children's Medical Center in Dallas. In
1998 Reivers Press in San Diego, California published I Miss My
Little Brother. The book is distributed by the Children's
Bereavement Center of South Texas, made available to the other
127 grief centers in the U.S., and is used to help both parents and
children understand the feelings of childhood grief.

2   Sometimes as I walked the halls of the Pediatric Intensive Care Unit
at Methodist Hospital and talked with parents and grandparents
about their seriously ill children, I found it easy to reach out, hold
a hand or touch a shoulder – sometimes take a distraught parent
into my arms as they let their pain erupt. At times like this I felt my
pain being swallowed up in their pain. I had walked where they
walked.

The publisher and author would love to hear your comments about this book.

To reach the author: email Jwilliams56@SATXrn.com, or go to her website, www.Darcystreasures.com

To reach the publisher, email Courtney@bookpros.com

Your comments will be valued.